Symphony No. 4
in C Minor, D417
"Tragic"

Edited by Johannes Brahms
from the Breitkopf & Härtel Complete Works Edition

Franz Schubert

DOVER PUBLICATIONS, INC.
Mineola, New York

M1001
,S375
D.417
2002x

0 50681518

Published in Canada by General Publishing Company, Ltd., 895 Don Mills
Road, 400-2 Park Centre, Toronto, Ontario M3C 1W3.
Published in the United Kingdom by David & Charles, Brunel House,
Forde Close, Newton Abbot, Devon TQ12 4PU.

Bibliographical Note

This Dover edition, first published in 2002, is an unabridged republication
of music from Serie I: "Symphonien für Orchester" of *Franz Schubert's Werke.
Kritisch durchgesehene Gesammtausgabe,* originally published by Breitkopf &
Härtel, Leipzig, 1884–5.

International Standard Book Number: 0-486-42135-X

Manufactured in the United States of America
Dover Publications, Inc., 31 East 2nd Street, Mineola, N.Y. 11501

CONTENTS

The word 'Tragische' was added on the title page of the symphony by Schubert himself, but at a later date. The third movement is entitled 'Minuetto' in Schubert's manuscript; this designation is missing in the Complete Works edition. The "D" number refers to an entry in *The Schubert Thematic Catalogue,* complied by Otto Erich Deutsch in collaboration with Donald R. Wakeling, Dover, 1995 (0-486-28685-1).

Symphony No. 4
in C Minor, D417
"Tragic"

Completed 27 April 1816

First public performance:
19 November 1849 / Buchhändlerbörse, Leipzig

INSTRUMENTATION

2 Flutes [Flauto]
2 Oboes [Oboi]
2 Clarinets in B♭ [Clarinetti in B]
2 Bassoons [Fagotti]

4 Horns in C, E♭, A♭ [Corni in C, Es, As]
2 Trumpets in C, E♭ [Trombe in C, Es]

Timpani

Violins I, II [Violino]
Viola
Cello & Bass [Violoncello e Basso]

I.

Adagio molto.

Flauto I.

Flauto II.

Oboi.

Clarinetti in B.

Fagotti.

Corni in C.

Corni in Es.

Trombe in C.

Timpani in C. G.

Violino I.

Violino II.

Viola.

Violoncello e Basso.

1

30

Allegro vivace.

46

54

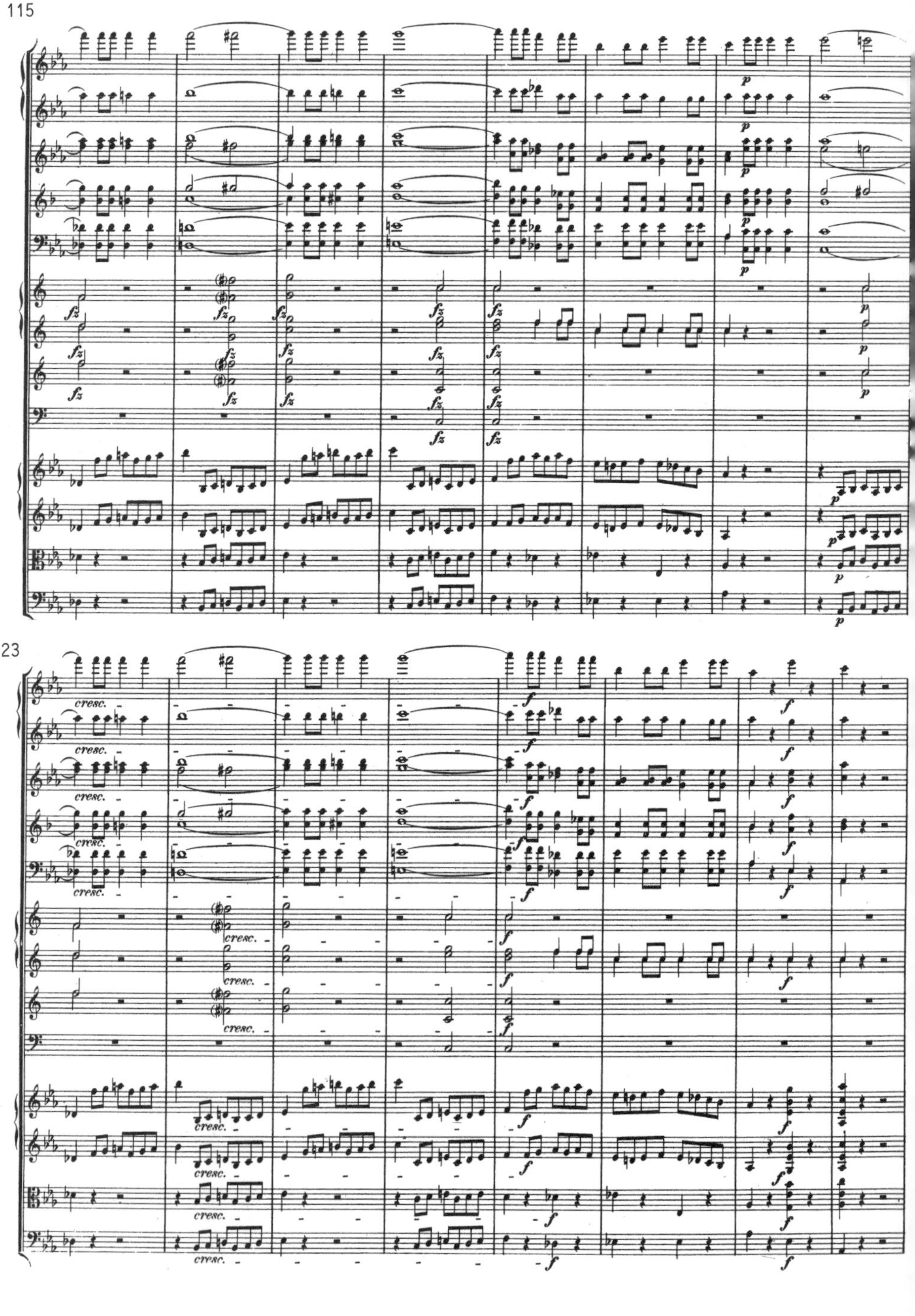
115
p
fz
p
fz
cresc.
f
123

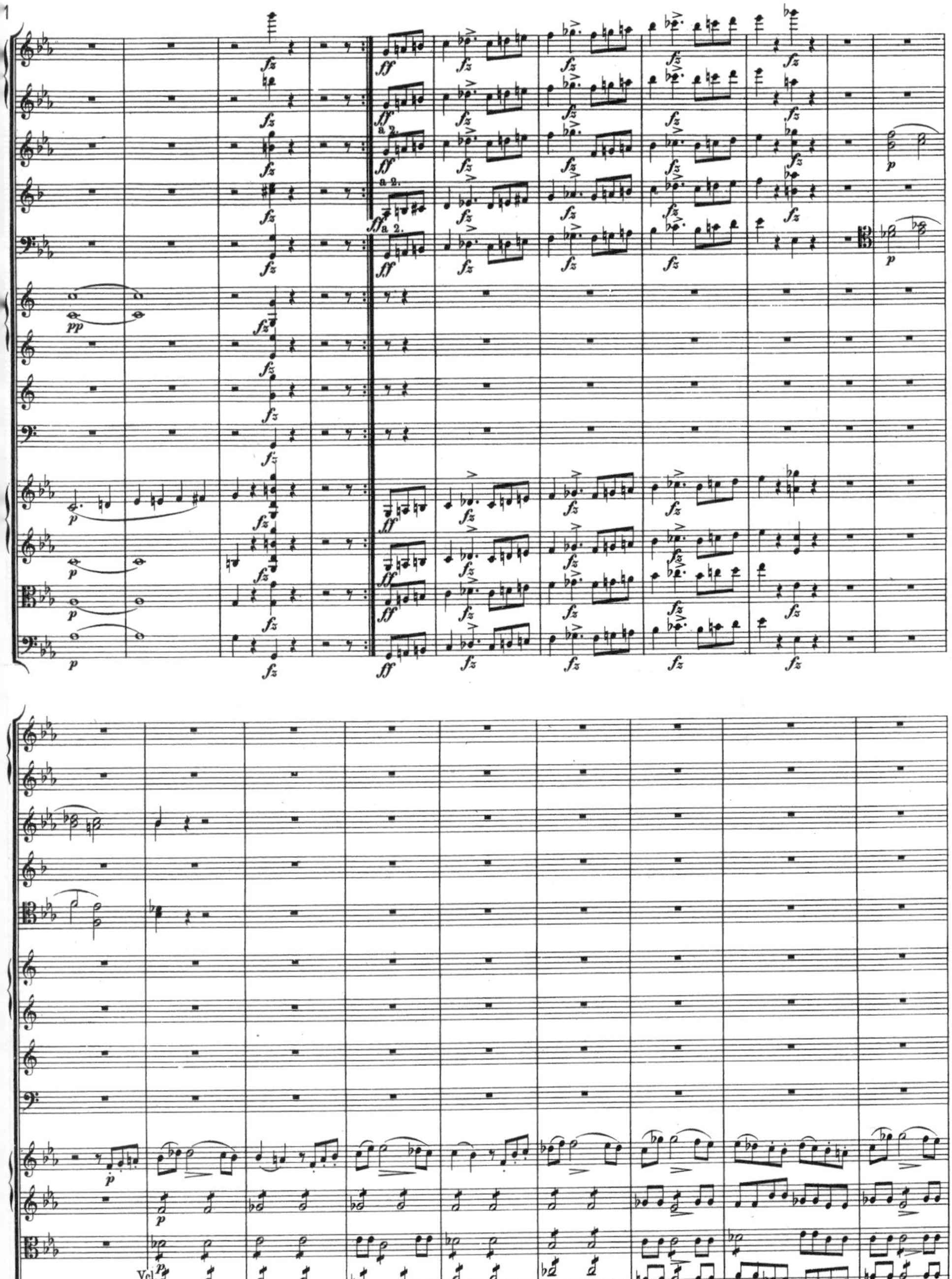
a 2.
a 2.
a 2.
Vcl.

150

158

182

190

214

224

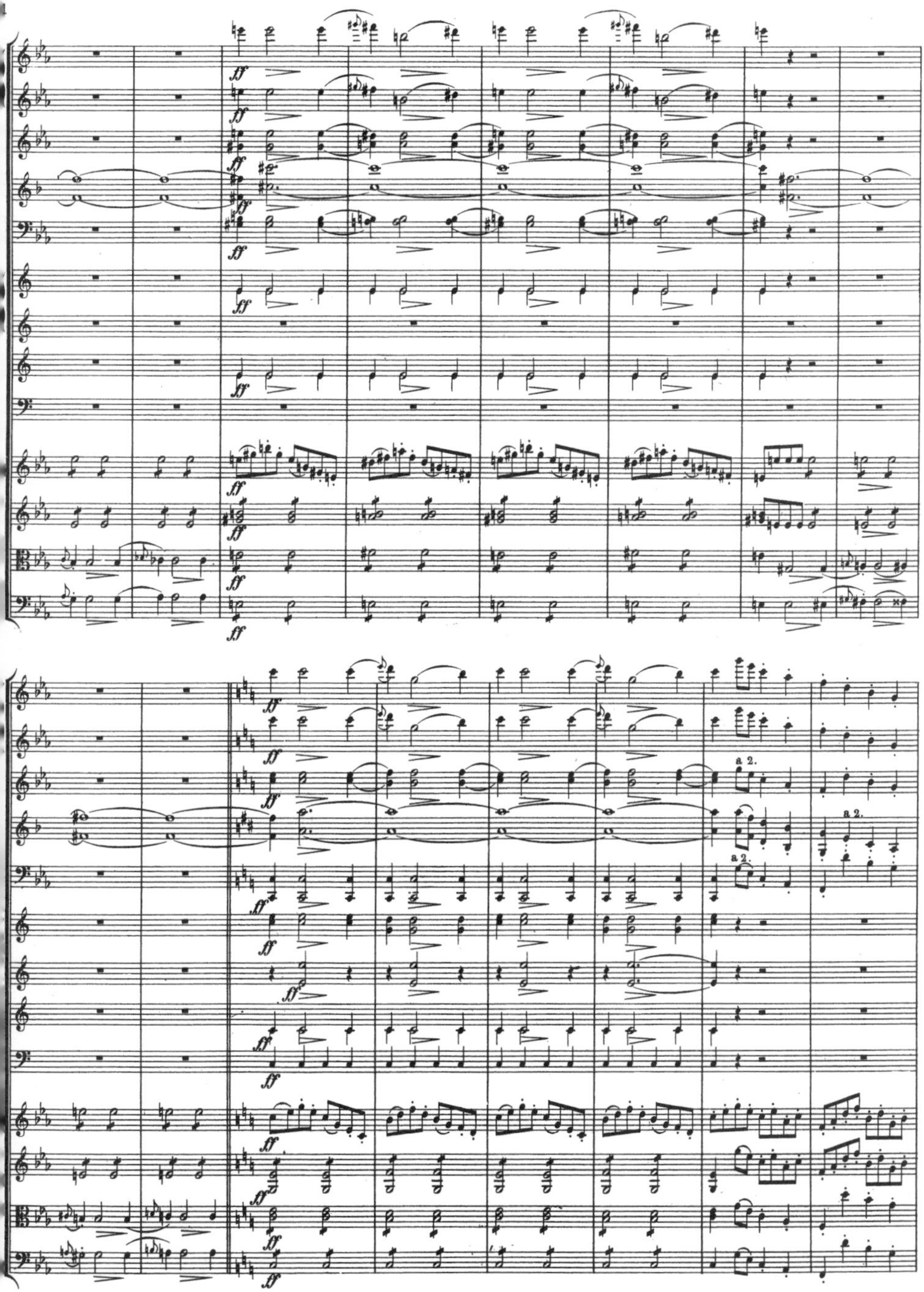
a 2.
a 2.
a 2.

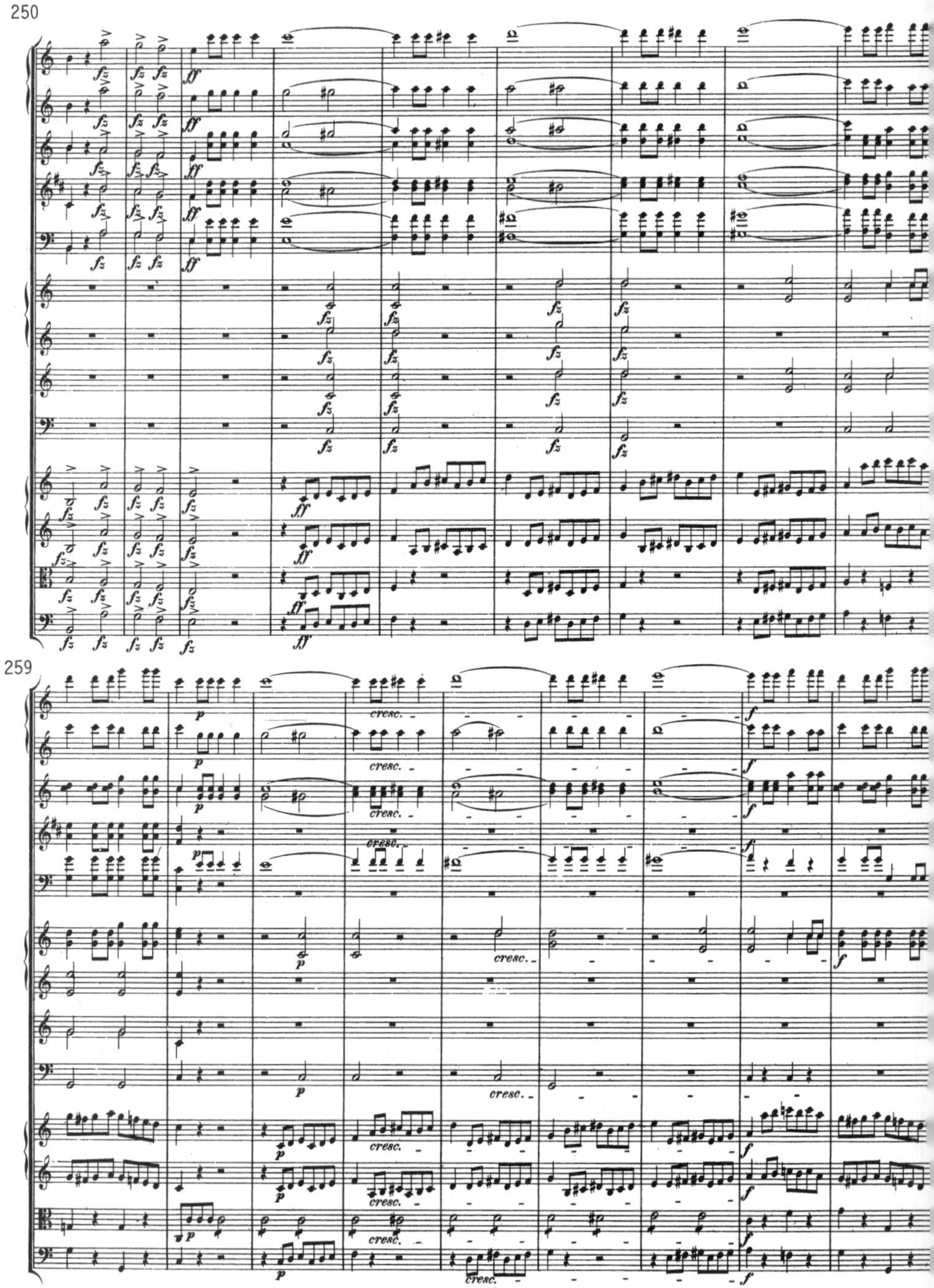
250
fz
ff
fz
259
p
cresc.
f

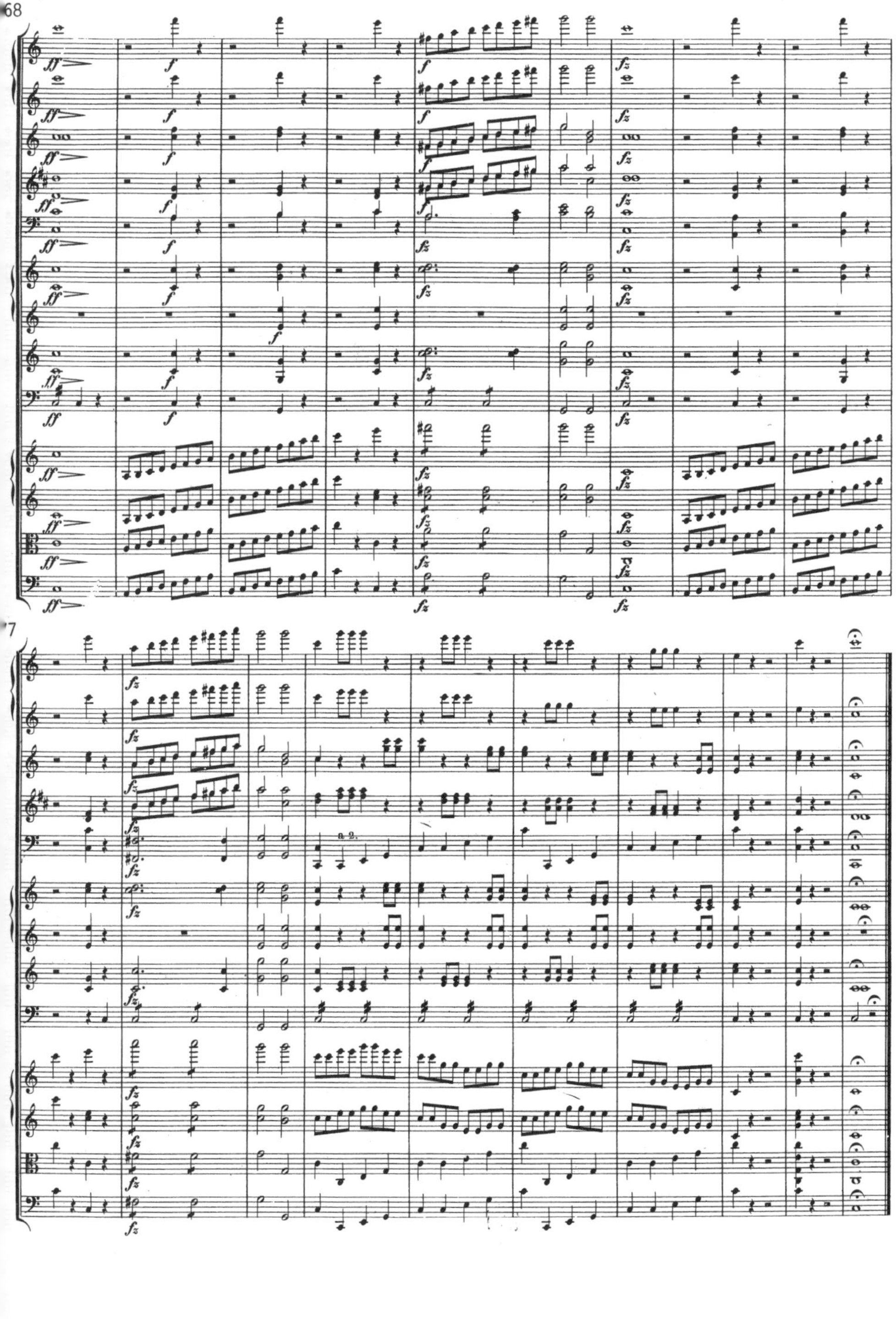
68
a 2.

II.

Flauto I.
Flauto II.
Oboi.
Clarinetti in B.
Fagotti.
Corni in As.
Violino I.
Violino II.
Viola.
Violoncello e Basso.

12

18

122

133

204

212

236

244

III.

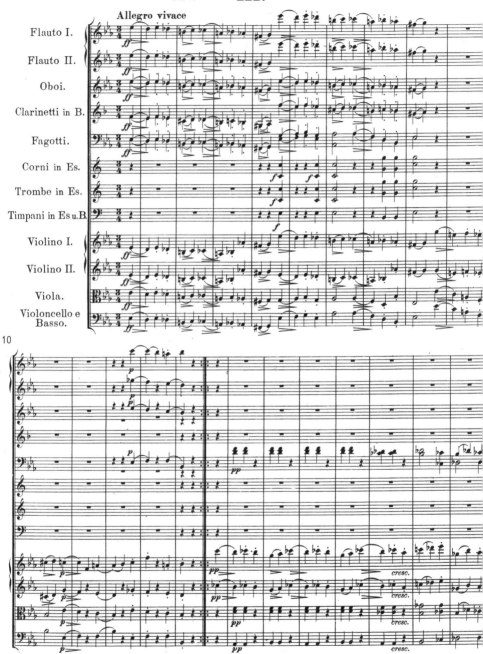

Allegro vivace

Flauto I.

Flauto II.

Oboi.

Clarinetti in B.

Fagotti.

Corni in Es.

Trombe in Es.

Timpani in Es u. B.

Violino I.

Violino II.

Viola.

Violoncello e Basso.

10

Men. D. C.

IV.

115

127

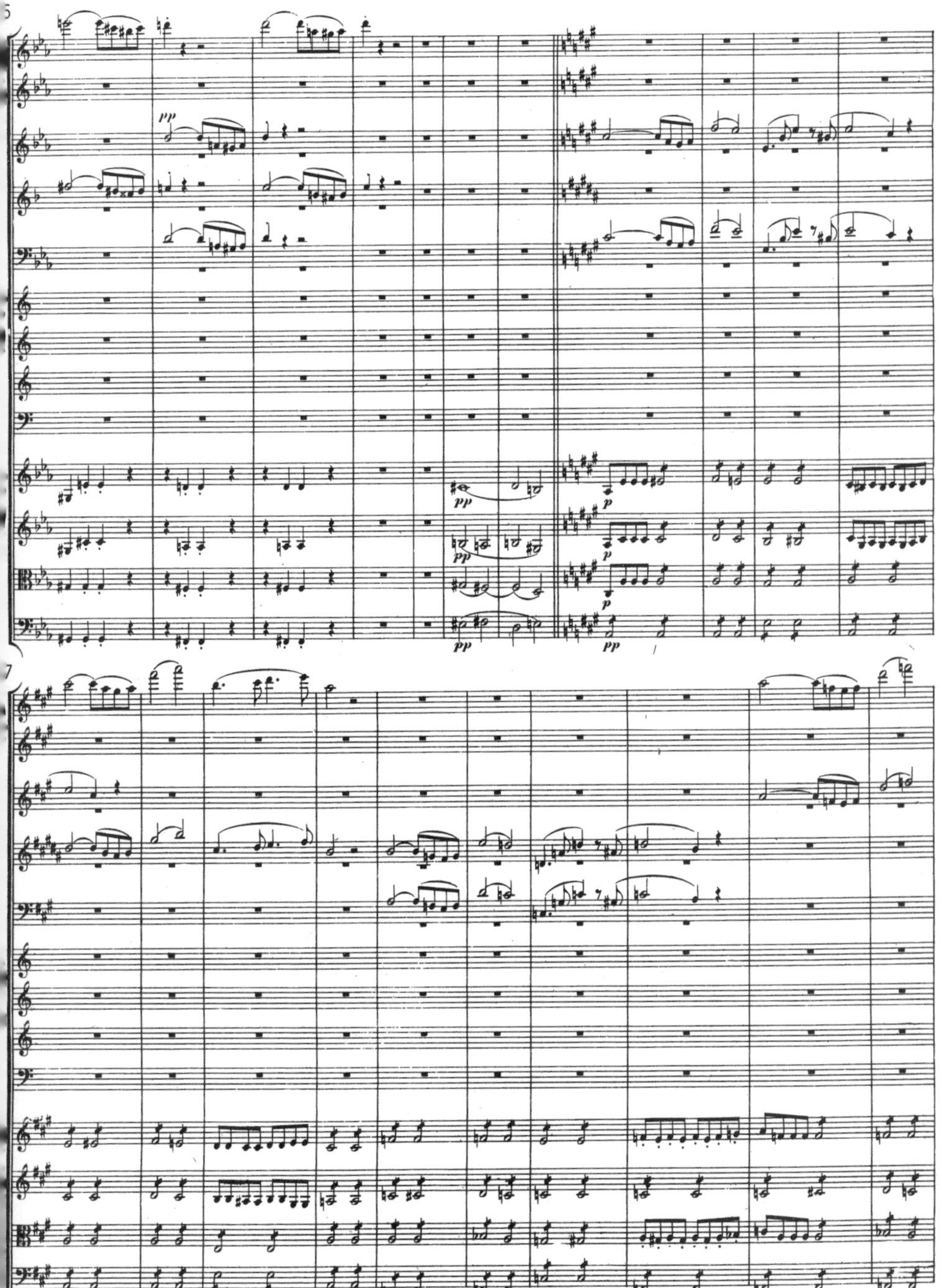
pp
pp
pp
pp
p
p
p
pp

237

246

312

323

425

434